0069414

D0947096

DATE DUE

FEB. 1 8 1994	
APR. 4 1994	
MAY 2 1994	
AUG 0 2 1994	
JAN 1 3 1997	
MAR 0 3 1997	
JUN 1 7 1997	
NOV 1 3 1997	

GV
1493
T686
1992

Townsend, Charles
  Barry.

World's hardest
  puzzles.

$12.95

World's
Hardest
Puzzles

Charles Barry Townsend

Sterling Publishing Co., Inc.   New York

Dedication

This book is dedicated to the terrific kids I was fortunate enough to grow up with in the greatest of all small towns, Glen Ridge, New Jersey. In particular, I send my best wishes to Bill Coggins, Joan Edland, Vinny Enright, Helen Gilbert, Marilyn Meyer, Jay Mills, Anthony Moran, Tom Supplee, and Jack Van Wagoner.

In sorrow, I also dedicate this book to two old friends who have left us all too soon—John Mortimer and Tony Rossney.

Edited by Jeanette Green
with assistance from Vladimir Péan

Library of Congress Cataloging-in-Publication Data

Townsend, Charles Barry.
  World's hardest puzzles / by Charles Barry Townsend.
     p.   cm.
  Includes index.
  ISBN 0-8069-8516-X
  1. Puzzles.   I. Title.
  GV1493.T686 1992   91-41544
  793.73—dc20   CIP

10 9 8 7 6 5 4 3 2 1

Published in 1992 by Sterling Publishing Company, Inc.
387 Park Avenue South, New York, N.Y. 10016
© 1992 by Charles Barry Townsend
Distributed in Canada by Sterling Publishing
% Canadian Manda Group, P.O. Box 920, Station U
Toronto, Ontario, Canada M8Z 5P9
Distributed in Great Britain and Europe by Cassell PLC
Villiers House, 41/47 Strand, London WC2N 5JE, England
Distributed in Australia by Capricorn Link Ltd.
P.O. Box 665, Lane Cove, NSW 2066
Manufactured in the United States of America
All rights reserved

Sterling ISBN 0-8069-8516-X

Contents

Introduction

Welcome once again to our growing collection of the world's outstanding puzzles. This is our fifth book for Sterling Publishing, and we've made it the most challenging one to date. Since we know that the tougher the problem is, the better you like it, we've included some of the hardest brain-busters in our collection. We've also been able to scout out unusual and, at times, downright weird illustrations for our problems. The puzzles deal with flour and boats, antiques and chickens, dumbbells and rugs, hopscotch and bread. We've included most everything but the kitchen sink—and we're working on that.

From time to time, I receive letters from teachers who tell me how much they enjoy using the puzzles in our books to enliven their classrooms. It's nice to know that we're doing our bit for education. We would also like to thank all of the many readers who have made this puzzle collection possible.

And now, it's time for you to turn the page, "rev" up your brain waves, and tune in on our first puzzle, which, appropriately enough, deals with old-time radio. I can faintly hear the "Puzzle Answer Man Show" coming out of the Stromberg-Carlson now!

Charles Barry Townsend

Puzzles

World's Hardest "Radio" Puzzle

"All right, Mr. Puzzle Answer Man, let's see you answer this one:

> A word I know
> Six letters it contains;
> Subtract just one
> And twelve you'll find remains.

What is that word?"

In 1930s radio, the Puzzle Answer Man was very popular. Can you help him prove that six minus one equals twelve? If you succeed, pay yourself one shiny, silver dollar, the standard radio prize in those days.

World's Hardest "Checkbook" Puzzle

"Could you please get me a pot of coffee, Ms. Upshot. I fear that I'm going to be up all night trying to reconcile this confounded checkbook."

```
Beginning balance for the month... $54.00
Check #0221    $20.00     Balance    $34.00
Check #0222    $20.00     Balance    $14.00
Check #0223    $10.00     Balance    $ 4.00
Check #0224    $ 4.00     Balance    $  .00
=========================================
       Total   $54.00         Total   $52.00
```

Thaddeus Tightwad has been trying for hours to figure out why the two sides of his checkbook ledger are not the same. Can you determine where the missing two dollars have gone?

World's Hardest "Checkerboard" Puzzle

Cy Corncrib will be pulling out his goatee if he loses one more game of checkers to Pop Bentley. He hasn't won since Hoover was President. Shown above is the ending of their last match. Pop was playing the white pieces and it was his turn. The white pieces move up the board while the black move down. What devious moves did Pop make to seal Corncrib's fate?

World's Hardest "Plywood" Puzzle

Our local handyman, Hiram Ballpeene, just returned from his reunion at Carpentry College where he stumped everyone with his new plywood puzzle. He showed them a piece of wood composed of five equal squares. First you must make two straight cuts across the panel, dividing it into three pieces. Then fit these pieces together so that they form a perfect square. How did Hiram do it?

World's Hardest "Western" Puzzle

This looks like a high-noon shoot-out in Dodge City. However, there's something odd about their conversation. Did Skinner forget to water down the Redeye, or have they been out in the sun too long? What do you think caused their highfalutin' repartee?

World's Hardest "Line" Puzzle

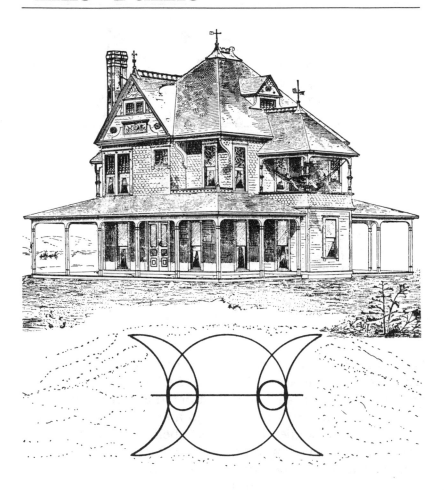

Amos Edelhagen is napping in his hammock when he should be out on the beach, enjoying his vacation. It seems that he spent all morning on the beach drawing in the sand, attempting to solve a line problem. He wanted to draw the above figure, using just one continuous line without letting any part of the line cross any other part of the line. Truly a puzzle to ruin anyone's vacation!

World's Hardest "Flour" Puzzle

While checking his supplies, Cy Corncrib noticed something interesting about his flour sacks. The sacks were
stacked three to a shelf and numbered one through nine.
On shelves one and three, he had a single sack next to a
pair of sacks, while the middle shelf held three sacks
grouped together. Now, if he multiplied the number on the
single sack (7), by the number on the pair next to it (28),
he got 196, the number on the middle sacks. However, if he
tried multiplying the numbers on the third shelf, (34) and
(5), he got 170.

Cy then came up with this problem: How do you rearrange the sacks, with as few moves as possible, so that
when you multiply each pair by its single neighbor, you
will come up with a product equal to the number on the
middle shelf?

World's Hardest "Animal" Puzzle

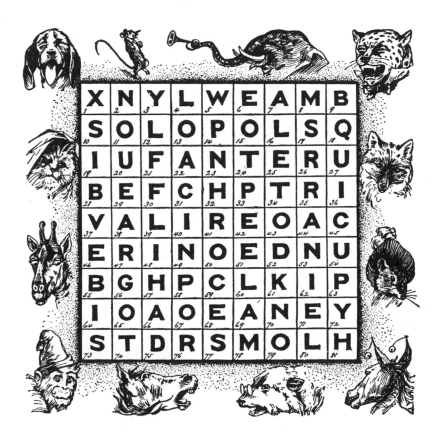

The eighty-one squares in the puzzle picture contain the names of forty-four animals. They may be spelled out by what is known in chess as the "King's Move," namely, one square at a time in any direction. Thus, from the first *O* on the second line, you could move to *X*, *N*, *Y*, *L*, *F*, *U*, *I* or *S*. Thus, *DOG* might be found in the squares 75, 65, 56; and *PORCUPINE* in 33, 43, 35, 45, 54, 63, 62, 70, and 71. Perseverance is necessary if you hope to find all forty-four animals.

World's Hardest "Glass" Puzzle

J. Wellington Moneybags, the Prince of Gamblers, is back with a "glass" stumper. Place two inverted glasses close enough together so that you can prop a stick match between them about halfway up, as shown. Now, Wellington will bet that he can remove *one* glass and the match will remain suspended in air. You may not touch the match with anything other than the second match on the table, and you must do that prior to removing the glass. Anyone care to wager?

World's Hardest "Boating" Puzzle

On a sunny Sunday afternoon, the Bennington girls left the east shore of Greasy Bear River in their new tri-motor skiff and headed for the opposite shore. At the same moment, the Davenport brothers left the west shore of the river in their racing shell and headed towards the opposite shore. One of these boats was travelling much faster than the other. The boats passed each other in the river 410 feet from one shore. Both boats continued until they reached the opposite shores.

Each crew spent an hour ashore, then headed back across the river for home. Once again the boats passed each other in their travels. This time they were 230 feet from one of the river banks.

Using the above information, can you calculate the width of the river?

World's Hardest "Paper" Puzzle

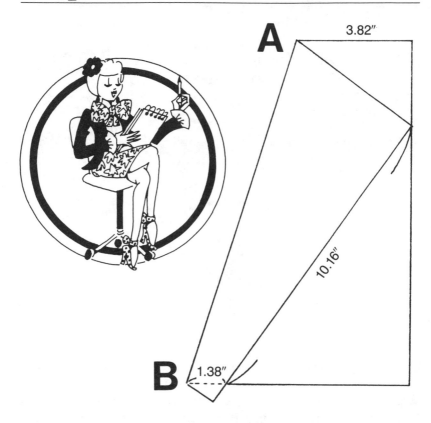

Harriet is not only the prettiest woman in the secretarial pool, she's also the best puzzler in the office. One day, when the boss's son challenged her to prove how good she was at puzzles, she took out a sheet of 8½-by-11-inch typing paper, folded it once, and marked some measurements on it.

"All right, Herbert, I'll bet you lunch that you can't calculate the length of the fold (A–B) without measuring it. I've marked down three lengths on the paper. This is all the information you'll need to solve this simple problem."

Can you succeed where Herbert failed?

World's Hardest "Division" Puzzle

> "Well, students, I see by the teaching guide that you are working on division problems this week. Let's see just how far you've progressed. On the board I've written a problem in long division. To make it more difficult, I've substituted X's for all of the numbers except the lucky 7's. It's your job to reason out what these numbers were and to write them back into the expression. You have until the end of the period to solve this one."

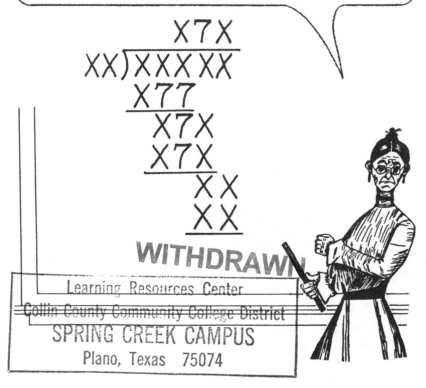

Ms. Priscilla Sunshine is once again our substitute teacher for the day. Make sure that your erasers are handy.

World's Hardest "Hardware" Puzzle

Last Sunday, down at Tutwyler's Hardware Store, Ben was playing with the balance scale that Grandfather Tutwyler had brought over from the old country in 1903. After a while, Ben observed:

(1) Three nuts plus one bolt were equal in weight to twelve washers.
(2) One bolt was equal in weight to one nut plus eight washers.

Using this information, he came up with a puzzle—How many washers are equal in weight to one bolt?

World's Hardest "T" Puzzle

The gentleman here with the W. C. Fields nose is on his way to a "T"—not a Boston tea party, but a Puzzle "T" Party where he's to judge the entries. To enter, you must first make a letter "T" out of a piece of cardboard. It should be the same size as the one pictured here. Then cut the letter into four pieces, each piece being the same size and shape. Don't be snippy if you miss this one.

World's Hardest "Age" Puzzle

"Really, Madge, we've been seeing each other for over a year now. Don't you think that it's about time you told me your age?"

"Roger, only a cad would ask a young lady how old she is. However, to satisfy your morbid curiosity, I'll give you a hint:
I come from a very large family. Five years ago, I was five times as old as my youngest sister, Veronica. Today I'm only three times as old as she is. That's all the information you're going to get from me. And, knowing your prowess in mathematics, I'm sure my secret will remain closely guarded."

Can you help Roger discern Madge's true age?

World's Hardest "Chess" Puzzle

Over a hundred years ago, Kempelen's famous Automation Chess Player could not only beat most players that challenged it, but it could also formulate chess puzzles that stumped the best minds of the day. Here's one of the hardest. You are required to place four black queens and a black bishop on a chessboard so that they control the entire board. In other words, after the five pieces have been positioned, it will be impossible to place the white king on any vacant square without being in check.

World's Hardest "Card" Puzzle

Back in 1843 Professor Anderson, Wizard of the North, was the leading magician in Great Britain. On the night shown here, he was giving a soiree in card manipulation.

Holding thirteen different cards in his right hand, he began to spell out the names of the cards. First, he spelled out A-C-E. At each letter he removed the top card and placed it on the bottom of the deck facedown. After three cards had been transferred to the bottom, he turned over the next top card and placed it faceup on the table. It was an ACE. Next, he spelled out F-O-U-R the same way. The next card he turned over was a FOUR. He continued in a like manner until the only card left in his hand was a KING. Obviously, to do this trick, the cards had to be set up in a predetermined order. Your puzzle is to discern this order. Use the cards two through the ace once.

World's Hardest "Antique" Puzzle

Mercator Wins
$10,000 For
Antique Puzzle

Alex Mercator, proprietor of the Nothing New Antique Mart, is seen here happily reading the news of his unexpected win at last month's puzzle convention. He challenged the contest judges to take the seventeen antique items he brought with him and arrange them in four straight lines on the floor, with each line containing five items. Can you succeed where the eminent panel of experts failed?

World's Hardest "Archaeology" Puzzle

"Well, Petrie, there it is—Plato's Cube. They said it didn't exist, but our perseverance has paid off. According to Plato, the huge central cube was made up of many smaller marble cubes. Also, the square central plaza that it sits on is made of these same smaller cubes. On top of that, the plaza has the same number of smaller cubes in it as the huge central cube is made of."

"Quite right, Hawkings. For once, we're in agreement. Another point that you should note is that the length of one side of the plaza is exactly twice the length of one side of the cube, which brings us to the nature of Plato's puzzle. Without going over to the plaza, can you calculate how many smaller cubes were used in building both the cube and the plaza? Although there are several answers to this problem, we are looking for the one that uses the smallest number of cubes to satisfy all the rules of construction that we have related."

World's Hardest "Brick" Puzzle

Quick Stack McGee, the ace bricklayer at Branigan's Masonry Creations, has come up with an interesting example of Brick Bafflement. Quick Stack puts six bricks on the ground and challenges his adversaries to arrange them so that every brick will touch three other bricks. There are two ways to solve this problem, and Quick Stack expects you to come up with both.

World's Hardest "Escape" Puzzle

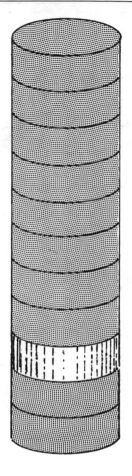

In this stack of wooden checkers, one lonely red checker is trapped beneath a column of black checkers. Your job is to free this imprisoned checker. In doing this, you may not touch the checkers in the stack with anything other than the single red checker pictured to the right of the stack. Also, you may not knock any of the checkers above or below the red checker off of the pile. The answer should be a snap for you.

World's Hardest "Number" Puzzle

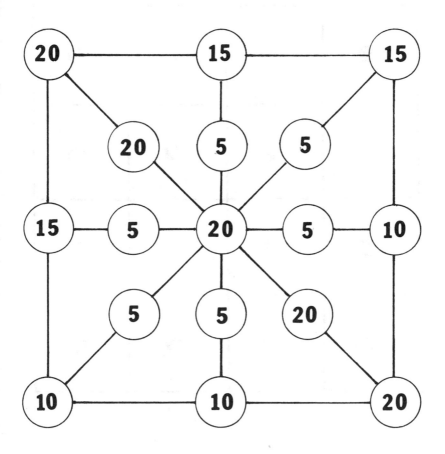

This is a rather neat number puzzle. You are challenged to rearrange the 17 numbers in this diagram so that they add up to 55 along any of the eight straight lines that make up the grid.

World's Hardest "Dots" Puzzle

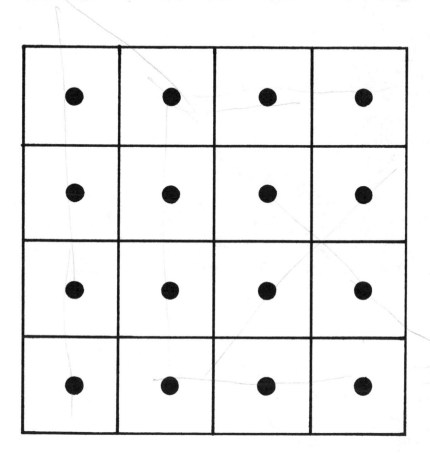

Draw the above sixteen-square grid on a separate sheet of paper, and place a dot in the middle of each square. Now for the puzzle: Try to draw six straight lines that will pass through every dot in the grid—without lifting the pencil from the paper. Here's a slight hint: you will have to pass through two of the dots twice. Also, your first line must start outside the grid.

World's Hardest "Castle" Puzzle

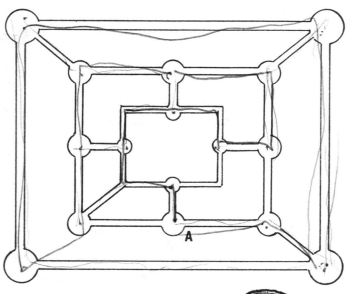

Shown above is the layout of the battlements of the ancient Raynham Castle. Every hour the stalwart guard, Edwin of York, made his rounds. He began at the turret marked *A*, and visited each of the sixteen

turrets, assuring that all was well. He did not double back during his inspection nor did he enter any turret more than once. At the end of his tour, Edwin returned to his starting point. Can you map out his route?

World's Hardest "Rebus" Puzzle

> 2 B ALWAYS
> E co X nf Aid Men S t
> I d S i H m ES
> 111 chances T 4 H 6 E s M

Our Victorian puzzler is working on one of the hardest rebus problems anywhere. The advice to students, once deciphered, will prove as apt today as it was a hundred years ago.

World's Hardest "Poet" Puzzle

> And sundry denizens of the air
> Are flying, aye each to his nest;
> And eager make at such an hour
> All haste to reach the mansions blest."
>
> "The sun is darting rays of gold
> Upon the moor, enchanting spot
> Whose purple heights by Ronald loved,
> Up open to his shepherd cot.

Our young bohemian poet is also something of a puzzler. Buried in each line of his poem are the names of famous British and American poets. As an example we've set in roman type the poet Felicia Dorothea *Hemans*'s name in the last line. Now it's your turn.

World's Hardest "Floating Paper" Puzzle

Last night at the Paper Mill Ball, betting achieved a fever pitch. Waldo Pennypacker, shown above, simultaneously dropped two sheets of writing paper from shoulder height. Which piece of paper will touch the floor first? Hundreds rode on each foot the paper fell. How could you ensure that paper *a* would land first? Of course, nothing could be attached to or added to either sheet of paper.

World's Hardest
"Paper Match" Puzzle

Between brews at the next Octoberfest, try stumping the local revelers with this Masterful Match Mystery. Lay out ten matches on the table and challenge anyone to arrange the matches to create five equilateral triangles. Hint: Some matches can form the side of more than one triangle.

World's Hardest "Magic Square" Puzzle

This gentleman is reading about the prize-winning magic square puzzle. To solve it, replace the X's in the grid with the correct numbers to create a square that adds up to 34 in each column, row, and the two major diagonals. Use numbers 1 through 16; no number may be used more than once.

World's Hardest "Soda Straw" Puzzle

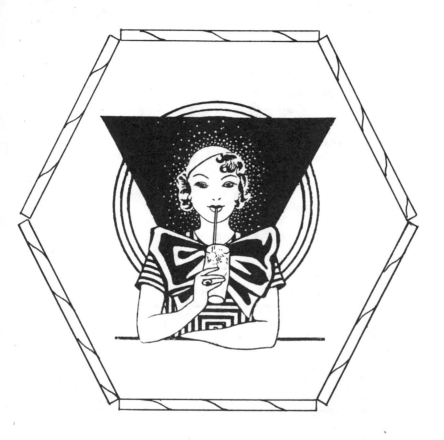

Soda Shop Sally has sipped many a free Seltzer Surprise, thanks to her puzzle-solving skills. She solved this problem in a quick, soda-pop fizz. Six soda straws were placed on the table in the form of a regular six-sided hexagon. The soda jerk challenged her to add three more straws and rearrange the nine straws to form another regular six-sided figure. Sally's time was less than 30 seconds; can you beat this?

World's Hardest "Newspaper" Puzzle

"Hello, Eddie, this is Horatio Stumpwell. Here's the copy for today's puzzle column:

'The Ancient sat and pondered well,
The following puzzle I'm about to tell.
From six you remove nine,
Now isn't that fine!
From nine you remove ten,
Don't try that again!
From forty you remove fifty,
That's what I call nifty!
A six is all that's left over,
Solve the puzzle and you'll be in clover.'

Rush that down to the printer!"

"Yes, sir, Mr. Stumpwell, I'm on my way!"

You're going to have to go back nearly 2,000 years to solve this one.

World's Hardest "Steamship" Puzzle

Back in the golden age of steam, great steamships entered and left New York Harbor on a daily basis. On one day, three ships cleared the Narrows and headed for Portsmouth, England. The first ship made the round trip to Portsmouth and back in 12 days. It took the second ship 16 days to complete the round trip. The third ship came limping back to New York in 20 days. Since the turnaround time in port was 12 hours, the ships were always back at sea the same day that they arrived. How many days will pass before all three ships again leave New York on the same date, and how many round trips will each ship make in the meantime?

World's Hardest "Typewriter" Puzzle

H
A
N
1. G

2. HEAD
   D

3. ONCE
   8AM

4. LO HEAD VE
   HEELS

5. DAYDAYOUT

6. sopBACTRIAN

7. Sympho

8. BED
   BED

The *doodle words* shown here represent a proper name, common saying, or familiar object. The first doodle word stands for "hang-up." If you got that one, it should be a cinch to solve the remaining seven.

World's Hardest "Gold Bar" Puzzle

Patrick O'Donald, the famous Nome gnome, spent days digging for gold and nights drinking at the Northern Lights Saloon. At the beginning of each month, Patrick cast his gold into a 31-inch-long bar. Every night he ate and drank the equivalent, in gold, of one inch of the bar. Instead of cutting the bar into 31 pieces, Patrick figured out the smallest number of pieces necessary to pay the bartender each night. The first night, for example, he gave the barkeep a one-inch piece; the second night, he paid with a two-inch piece and took back the one-inch piece. What are the fewest number of pieces he would need to cut the bar into so that he could get through any month of the year?

World's Hardest "Moon" Puzzle

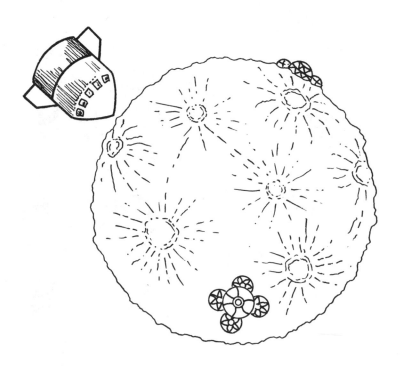

It's been rumored that NASA has drawn up plans to put several space stations on the moon in the near future. If each station must be the same distance away from every other station on the moon, what is the maximum number of stations that could be constructed on the moon's surface? You may need to reposition our two sample stations.

World's Hardest "Train" Puzzle

In 1879 ore trains leaving the Silverado Mine passed through Dead Dutchman Mountain on the way to the smelter's. The tunnel through Dead Dutchman was exactly one mile long, and the trains that hauled the ore were exactly one mile long from the cowcatcher on the lead locomotive to the red lantern hanging on the back of the caboose. If the ore train travelled at a steady 15 miles per hour, how long did it take the entire train to pass through the tunnel?

World's Hardest "Chicken" Puzzle

"But, Amy, I only had $24 at the end of the day!"

"Don't try to cheat me, Bessie. You owe me another 50 cents!"

Farming neighbors Amy and Bessie went to market every day to sell their chickens. Bessie sold 30 chickens a day, at two chickens for $1.00, and brought home $15.00. Amy sold 30 chickens a day, at three chickens for $1.00, and brought home $10.00. One day Amy was sick, so she asked Bessie to sell her chickens for her. Bessie took the 60 chickens to market and sold them all at the rate of five chickens for $2.00. She brought home a total of $24 for the day's work. This was a dollar less than the two women usually made each day when they sold their chickens separately. What happened to the extra dollar? Did Bessie pocket it?

World's Hardest "Progression" Puzzle

HOLE	1	2	3	4	5	6	7	8	9	TOTAL
Divots Davenport	4	5	5	6	3	4	5			
Sandy Bunker	12	9	3	6	3	1				

Sandy Bunker, one of Idle Hours Country Club's golf pros, is having a spotty day on the links. His score for the first six holes reads like a roller coaster. The funny thing is that Sandy's score, hole by hole, has been moving according to a set progression. Can you figure out what Sandy's score was on the seventh hole?

World's Hardest "Coin" Puzzle

"She'll being coming round the Alps when she comes, when she comes!"

TIP BUCKET

The Bellowing Bavarian Belters had another poor night at the local rathskeller. When they finished their last set, only a few American tourist coins lay in the tip bucket. Rudi commented that with these coins he could pay the exact amount for anything costing from one cent to one dollar. He also said that the group had the smallest number of coins that you could do this with. What coins were in the bucket?

World's Hardest "Clairvoyant" Puzzle

Madame Olga knows all, sees all, and if you cross her palm with silver, or paper, she'll tell all. You too can be clairvoyant and fool your friends with your so-called powers. Stretch out your hand above the table, palm down, and ask someone to place a quarter on top of it, heads down. Bet them that by studying the tail side of the coin you can tell them the date. Before consulting the answer page for the method used to perform this feat, see if you can figure out how it's done.

World's Hardest "Logo" Puzzle

Posing here is Woo Ling Yu, advertising agent for the famous Spicy Tea Export Company. He has his arm around the company logo, a cross inside a square—a symbol recognized around the world. Many years ago, Woo created a puzzle with this logo. Using an oriental fountain brush, Woo claimed that he could draw the logo without lifting the brush from the paper and without going over any line more than once. Can you figure out how he did it?

World's Hardest "Dumbbell" Puzzle

"I say, Bertie, if you give me one of your dumbbells, I'll have twice as many dumbbells as you!"

"No, Basil, it's better if you give me one of your dumbbells. Then we'll both have the same number!"

The Balancing Bertolli Brothers were a class act. Strength and snappy puzzles were their specialty. They may have wowed them on the continent, but I don't think they would have done well in the colonies. Anyhow, can you figure out how many dumbbells Bertie and Basil each had?

World's Hardest "Rug" Puzzle

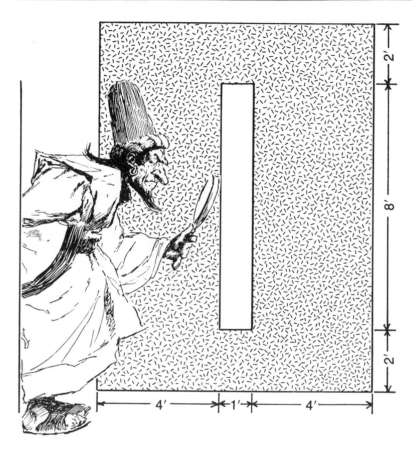

Abdul, the rug merchant, is in deep trouble. He has to deliver a ten-foot-by-ten-foot rug to a wealthy client by sundown. He planned to make it out of a piece of nine-foot-by-twelve-foot carpet in his warehouse, but when he unrolled the carpet, he found that someone had cut a one-foot-by-eight-foot piece out of its center. Quick as a genie, Abdul figured out a way to cut the rug into two pieces that could then be sewn back together to form a solid ten-foot-by-ten-foot rug.

World's Hardest "Gulliver" Puzzle

"We are little airy creatures,
  All of different voice and features;
One of us in 'glass' is set,
  One of us you'll find in 'jet',
T'other you may see in 'tin',
  And the fourth a 'box' within.
If the fifth you should pursue,
  It can never fly from 'you'."

Gulliver here is entertaining the Queen of Lilliput with Jonathan Swift's puzzle poem. The problem involves figuring out the five "little airy creatures" the poem describes.

World's Hardest "Lawn" Puzzle

Our neighbors have a pet ram, Amos, that they keep tethered to the corner of their house. They have a square house which measures 30 feet on each side. The tether on Amos is 60 feet long, which allows him to graze over a large part of their property—back, front, and sides. Can you calculate the maximum number of square feet of lawn Amos can reach for grazing?

World's Hardest "Political" Puzzle

P	T	P	Y	E	L
D					C
I					E
N					A
T					R
A	O	E	O	O	N
					T

Election years in the United States seem to always have encouraged wild rhetoric and slogans. We've taken one of the most famous political slogans and made it into a puzzle. See if you can read the slogan in the frame of letters above. Beginning with any letter, go around the frame twice, reading every other letter as you go. You'll be up a creek if you miss this one!

World's Hardest "Clock" Puzzle

Waldo Snoozingham fell asleep while reading *War and Peace*. Sometime later he was awakened by hearing one chime from his downstairs clock. His clock strikes once every quarter-hour and gives a full number of chimes on the hour. Since Waldo was too tired to get up, how long would he have to sit in his cozy chair until he could be sure of the right time? There are two possible answers to this puzzle.

World's Hardest "Math" Puzzle

"This, Dryden, is my entry for this year's Mystery Number Contest!"

"Frankly, Boswell, after looking over your addition problem, I see nothing mysterious about it!"

986
818
969
989
696
616
5,074

Can you figure out what makes this contest entry unique?

World's Hardest "Toy Box" Puzzle

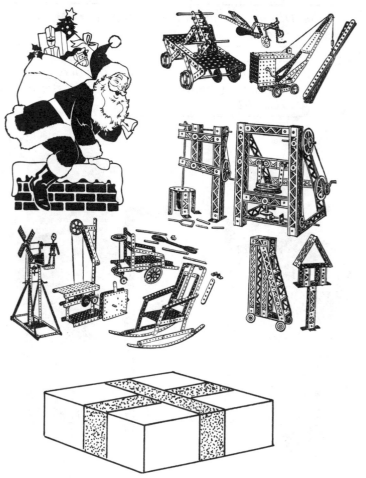

Before the invention of the silicon chip, building blocks and construction toys were among children's favorite Christmas gifts. The items shown here were built with materials that came in a box with these measurements: the top—120 square inches, the side—96 square inches, and the end—80 square inches. Can you figure out the length, width, and height of the box?

World's Hardest "Punctuation" Puzzle

"Come on, Jimmy, go back inside and apologize to your teacher!"

"It was and I said not are and and and are are different!"

It looks as though Jimmy's in a lot of trouble with his substitute teacher, Ms. Sunshine. We've made a puzzle out of his response to his buddy, Knuckles. Can you correctly punctuate what Jimmy said so that it makes sense?

World's Hardest "Sports" Puzzle

1. TRUCEOQ
2. ORCSEC
3. ICOBEC
4. TALFOLOB
5. LOLBVALYEL
6. NSIETN
7. SALSEROC
8. CARGIN
9. LEEHTSEEPCAS
10. OTSNOHGI
11. RCRYAEH
12. DOGBEBDLSNI
13. KYOCHE
14. GLASNII
15. SGTKANI
16. HGSFIIN
17. NKIBGI
18. LIBLGOAONN
19. LEBLBAAS
20. TUOIQS
21. BADLNAHL
22. BGUYR
23. TCEKICR
24. MSGIWMIN

In this puzzle we salute the wonderful world of sports. Below the names of 24 outdoor games are listed, but the letters have been scrambled. To win the match, you have ten minutes to unscramble them.

World's Hardest "Balancing" Puzzle

Here we find Tree-Tall Bentley trying to solve an old match-balancing puzzle. The problem is to drop a paper match, from waist level, to the ground and have it land on its narrow side edge, *not* on its flat sides. So far, Bentley hasn't found the secret to this seemingly impossible feat. Try the puzzle to see if you can light upon a solution before resorting to the answer section.

World's Hardest "Word" Puzzle

"I say, Livermore, is this really the man you claim to be the world's most intelligent waiter?"

"Quite right, Doubtington, and I'll prove it to you. Barlowe, how would you say to Mr. Doubtington here, in one word, that he had a late dinner between nine and eleven o'clock?"

"That's an easy one, sir. The word that I'd use is . . . !"

Can you serve the answer before it's time to pay the check?

World's Hardest "King" Puzzle

"So, you think that I've had trouble with women! Well, I'm not the only ruler who has run afoul with the so-called weaker sex. Let's see if you can fathom the name of this famous king from this little ditty.

'Five hundred begins it, five hundred ends it,
Five in the middle is seen;
The first of all figures, the first of all letters,
Take up their stations between.
Join all together, and then you will bring
Before you the name of an eminent king.'"

World's Hardest "Racing" Puzzle

Here is Professor Betsalot, that avid horse player. He's studying the racing form for the next race and has narrowed the field to three horses: Sway Belly at 4 to 1, Aunt Sara at 3 to 1, and Thunder Hooves at 2 to 1. The professor is trying to figure out how much he must bet on each horse so that he will win $13, no matter which of the three horses comes in first.

For example, if he bets $5 on each horse and Sway Belly wins, he'll win $20 on Sway Belly and lose $10 on the two other horses. See if you can solve the professor's problem before the race begins.

World's Hardest "Barrel" Puzzle

This is the story of one Gottlieb the Guzzler, a backwoods purveyor of wine and spirits. It seems that one day he bought an odd lot of merchandise that included five barrels of wine and one barrel of beer. Gottlieb, being a suds man, kept the barrel of beer and sold off the wine. Part of the wine he sold to the owner of Ye Olde Ale House and *twice* that amount to banker Rumport, a connoisseur of fine wines. This finished off the five barrels. None of the barrels had to be opened for these transactions. The barrels are clearly marked in the illustration with the number of gallons each contains. Can you figure out which barrel contained the beer, which barrels were sold to Ye Olde Ale House, and which ones were sold to banker Rumport?

World's Hardest "Nationality" Puzzle

"So tell me, Myra, who had the most difficult pair of hands you ever worked on?"

"So ask me a hard one, why don't you! Last week a little old Oriental woman came into the shop. I thought the gloves she wore were ten sizes too big before she took them off. Her nails were a foot long if they were an inch. I must have used a whole bottle of nail polish on them when I was through. She told me that all the old women where she came from never cut their nails. It seems that she was . . . E, E, E."

Myra has some great cuticle stories, all right. She also likes to show off her puzzling ability as exemplified by her way of specifying the long-nailed lady's origin. Can you figure out what Myra meant when she said the lady was "E, E, E"?

World's Hardest "Route" Puzzle

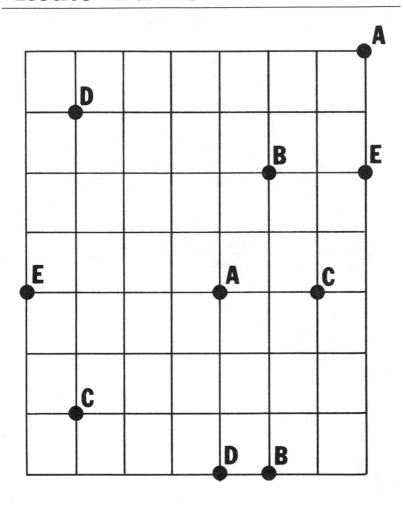

This is an old and rather interesting puzzle. On the grid above are five pairs of dots, labeled A through E. Connect these pairs: A to A, B to B, C to C, D to D, and E to E. The routes you lay out must follow the lines on the grid. No two routes may cross or touch each other. Now, take charge of traffic control.

World's Hardest "Inspirational" Puzzle

2b

a a a a a a a a a a
t C r I i O f U l S e s

standing
is the mark of a mean

On his way to vespers, the Reverend I. N. Spire pauses to study a rather cryptic inspirational message carved on a monument. The stonemason from long ago was something of a puzzler since he rendered advice in the form of a rebus. Can you solve the puzzle as quickly as the good reverend?

World's Hardest "Backwards" Puzzle

Sports, sports, sports! In the television age, we have been inundated by the many ways people, throughout the world, amuse themselves. In several sports, contestants win by travelling backwards. Name three such sporting activities.

World's Hardest "Odd Figure" Puzzle

The professors are in a stew at the Institute of ESP (Extra Sensory Puzzling). Someone submitted the problem for a solution, and they can't find it in the library.

Here it is: Write down five odd *figures* so that they add up to fourteen. See if you can solve the puzzle before the pepperoni arrives.

World's Hardest "Hopscotch" Puzzle

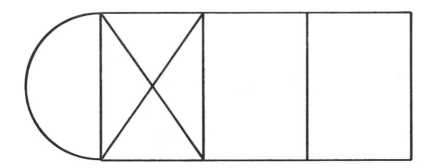

Here we see a group of 19th century lads passing time with a lively game of hopscotch. Under the illustration is a "puzzlescotch" pattern. To solve this puzzle, trace these puzzlescotch chalk marks using one continuous line without lifting your pencil from the paper and without crossing over any part of the line. Also, you may not go over any part of the line more than once. Don't skip to the answer section before trying this game.

World's Hardest "Wooden Match" Puzzle

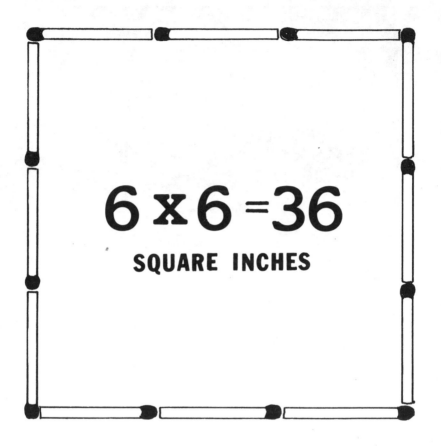

6 x 6 = 36

SQUARE INCHES

Here are twelve wooden matches arranged in a square. Each match is two inches long, which gives us a square measuring 6 inches by 6 inches. So, the matches enclose a 36-square-inch area. Rearrange these twelve matches into a new shape that will enclose an area of 12 square inches.

World's Hardest "Circle" Puzzle

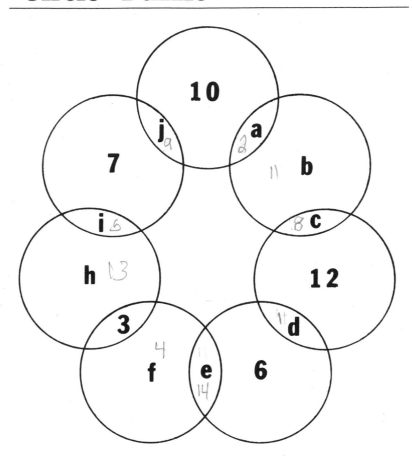

You may find yourself "seeing circles" before you finish this puzzle. The figure above is composed of seven interlocking circles. There are fourteen enclosed areas within the drawing. Replace the letters in the drawing with numbers so that all numbers from 1 to 14 will appear in the drawing. The puzzle involves doing this in such a way that the numbers within any one circle will add up to 21. There's no time limit on this one.

World's Hardest "Letter Dropping" Puzzle

The Grand Poobah from the Temple of Transcendental Puzzle Solving in California has dropped in to favor us with a "startling" challenge. From the word pictured above, G. P. wants you to drop one letter so that you have a new word. Then drop another letter, which in turn will leave you with yet another new word. Continue in this way until you have dropped all but one letter, and this last letter should also be a word. At no time may you rearrange any of the letters into a different order when forming each new word. Solve this one in two minutes, and you're eligible for a puzzle robe third-class.

World's Hardest "Bread" Puzzle

"This story is true! Clive told it to me himself. It seems that young Forsythe wandered away from Kitchener's army and became lost. Near starvation, he met two native chaps about to eat their midday meal. One chap had three loaves of bread and the other had five. They agreed to share their food with him if Forsythe paid for what he ate. Of course, he said yes, and all three ate equal shares of the eight loaves. When the meal was over, Forsythe gave them eight coins and eventually rejoined his regiment.

Meanwhile, the two natives fought over the money. The man with three loaves wanted the money divided equally, while the other chap wanted five coins for his share. This turned out to be quite a puzzle. How would you, ladies, have fairly divided the coins?"

World's Hardest "Roller" Puzzle

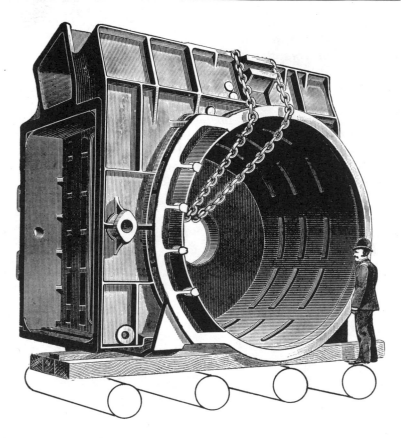

Here we see the flange assembly of a new air-conditioning unit being installed in the Roma All-Nite Pizza Parlor in midtown Manhattan. When you're baking up to one thousand pizzas an hour, you have to contend with a lot of hot air. The flange assembly was so heavy that they were forced to use steel cylindrical bars seven inches in diameter to move it. This brings us to our puzzle. After these bars have made one complete revolution, how far forward will the unit have moved? I think I'll have a slice while you're working on this one.

World's Hardest "Safe" Puzzle

At the turn of the century, a Hall's safe offered the ultimate protection for valuables. The safe shown here was owned by Timoney O'Shay, a man of great wealth who had a short memory. For the life of him, he couldn't remember the three numbers of the safe's combination. However, he had these clues pasted on top of the safe to help jog his memory:

"Multiply the 1st number by 3 and the answer is all ones. Multiply the 2nd number by 6 and the answer is all twos. Multiply the 3rd number by 9 and the answer is all threes."

If the safecrackers above had stayed in school, they may have been able to turn those clues into cash. Can you make those old tumblers fall into place?

World's Hardest "Money" Puzzle

Freddy Fastcount, head teller at the Old Lumpock Bank, was proud of his puzzling ability and liked to stump his coworkers with problems concerning the coin of the realm. One day, Freddy put a stack of one hundred silver dollars on the table and challenged all those present to divide the coins into two piles, according to these rules: the first pile should contain enough coins so that one-fourth of the amount would be twenty coins more than one-sixth the number of coins in the second pile. Let's see if you can credit your account with a correct answer.

World's Hardest "Transposition" Puzzle

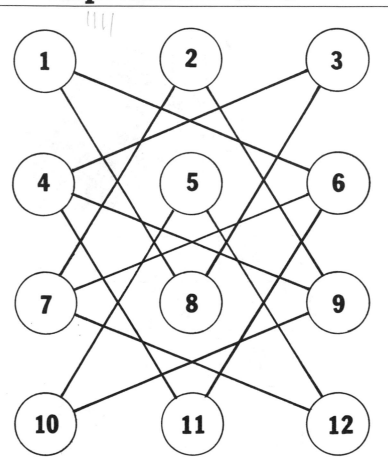

Here's a neat changing-places puzzle. Place three red checkers on positions 1, 2, and 3, and three black checkers on positions 10, 11, and 12. In just 22 moves, you must cause them to change places. Alternately move one checker at a time along the lines from one circle to another. At no time may a checker of one color be on a circle that a checker of the opposite color could reach on the next move. Only one checker may be on a circle at any one time.

World's Hardest "Poker Chip" Puzzle

The next time the cards are running against you and you're in a cold sweat, try this little puzzle to calm your nerves. Draw up a sixteen-square playing board similar to the one above and attempt to place ten poker chips in ten of the squares so that you form the greatest number of rows, with each row containing an even number of chips. The rows may be horizontal, vertical, or diagonal. Let's see how you stack up with this puzzle.

World's Hardest "Target" Puzzle

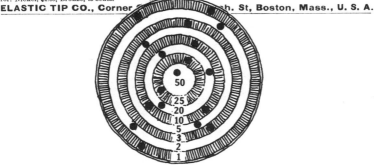

That turn-of-the-century fun family, the Oakleys, is back with another delightful target puzzle. Alexander and his sisters Sybilla and Swanhilda have each fired 6 shots at the target, and each one has scored 71 points. Now, Alexander's first two shots added up to 22 points and Swanhilda's first shot scored 3 points. See if you can tabulate the 18 shots to determine who hit the bull's-eye? Check the target for telltale evidence.

World's Hardest "Square" Puzzle

Here we see Fenton Catchall, Society Juggler, winding up his act with his famous Triangles-of-Death feat. Fenton holds no fear for the razor-sharp shards of steel. And, like the rest of the props in his act, they are derived from a famous puzzle. If you were to cut one of these five triangles in half, you could then take the resulting six pieces and fit them together to form a perfect square. Care to try your hand at this one?

World's Hardest "Baseball" Puzzle

In the 1950s two famous baseball teams fought a long and hard battle on the diamond. When the game was over, the home team won with a 1-to-0 victory over a far superior former world champion. The amazing thing about the victory was that no *man* had reached third base. The game was played according to the standard rules of baseball. Can you figure out how they managed to win the game?

World's Hardest "What?" Puzzle

"What occurs once in a second, once in a month, once in a century, but not at all in a week or a year?"

"What has a foot on each end and one in the middle?"

"What is black and white and has fuzz inside?"

"What is it that nobody wishes to have and nobody likes to lose?"

"What word will, if you take away the first letter, make you sick?"

World's Hardest "Moving" Puzzle

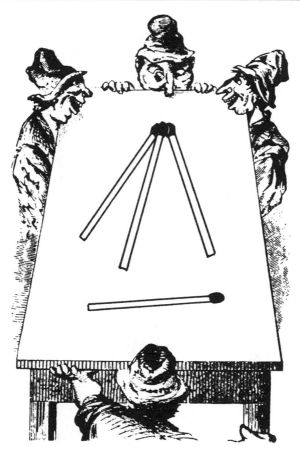

This puzzle should prove a moving experience. You'll need four wooden matches. Take three of the matches and balance them in the form of a pyramid, as shown above. Next, hand the fourth match to your victim. Challenge him to *lift* the three upright matches, using only the fourth match, transport them across the room, and place them on another table, still standing in pyramid form.

The old cronies down at the local hardware store have been working on it all afternoon.

World's Hardest "Cork" Puzzle

The cork from the "Bottle" Puzzle landed in Ms. Smedwick's water glass. It's strange but true that a cork will not stay in the center of a glass of water. Instead it will slowly drift over to the side of the glass, where it will remain. There is, however, a simple way to make the cork remain floating in the center of the glass. (Swirling the water is not the answer.)

World's Hardest "Bottle" Puzzle

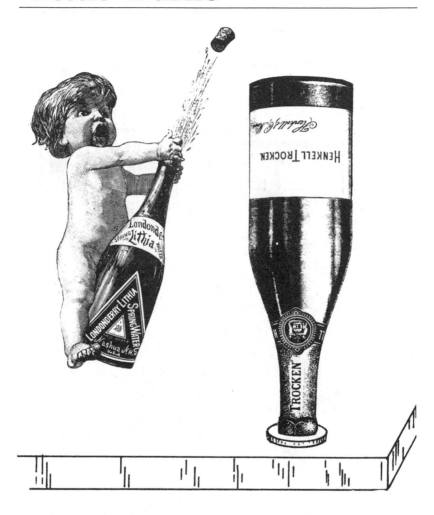

A bottle, preferably empty, and a nickel are all you need to present this puzzle. Place the nickel on the table, invert the bottle, and balance it on top of the coin. Now challenge friends to remove the coin from under the bottle without touching the bottle or knocking it over. You'll have them popping their corks trying to solve this one.

World's Hardest "Weighty" Puzzle

"Now, let's see, if you read this word forward, it's very, very heavy. However, if you read it backwards, it's not. Now how could that be? I'll probably be up all night trying to solve this one."

The old professor sat down for a night of light word puzzles and found himself in the middle of a tough one. Can you figure out what the overweight word is that the puzzler seeks?

World's Hardest "Rectangle" Puzzle

Mr. Gotrocks is mulling over the famous rectangle puzzle. The twelve black dots above are all evenly spaced from one another. How many rectangles, of varying sizes, can you find that would use any four of these dots for their vertices (corners)? Remember, a square is also considered a rectangle.

World's Hardest "Ballooning" Puzzle

Ballooning is one of the hottest new sports in the country. During a recent puzzle fair, ballooning became a new presentation category. Above is the winning entry of the Montgolfier brothers. Each brother piloted a balloon with four large words suspended beneath. Jacques's balloon is on the left and Joseph's is on the right. Determine which word suspended below the right balloon logically belongs with the four words under the left balloon? Anyone care to float a guess?

World's Hardest "Brothers" Puzzle

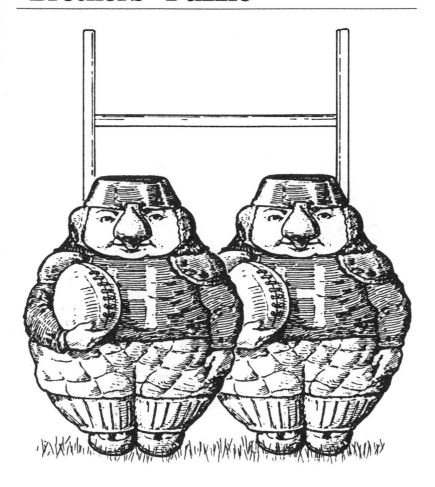

Back when football was really football, the Gunderson brothers were the best nose tackles on the Harvard team. The boys had the same father and mother and were born on the same day in the same hospital during the same year. As you can see, they look alike, but they're *not* twins. If you can work this puzzle within a minute, we'll give you two extra points.

World's Hardest "Suitcase" Puzzle

The Fabulous Frontenacs was one of the strangest musical acts of the century. Bertha and Reinhold played two instruments called the Berthaphone. Just before they began to play, Reinhold placed an old suitcase on a table. The suitcase hung slightly more than one-third over the table edge. They then launched into a medley of classical favorites. Sometime later, to everyone's surprise, the suitcase suddenly up-ended and tumbled to the floor. This closed their concert. No clockwork mechanization was inside the suitcase. Can you figure out how the Frontenacs timed their soirees?

World's Hardest "A to Z" Puzzle

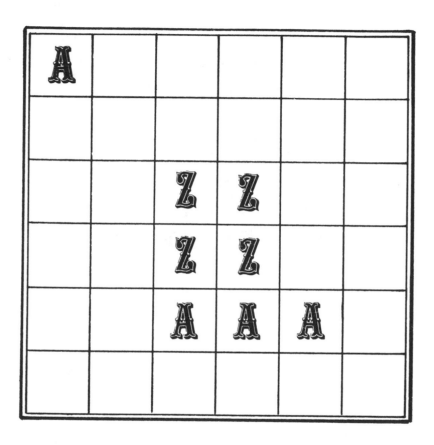

All right, puzzlers, it's time to tackle a really hard one. This six-by-six square grid contains four letter A's and four letter Z's. Cut this board into four pieces. All the pieces must be the same size and shape, and there must be one letter A and one letter Z in each of the pieces. You must cut the board along the grid lines. Good luck! You have one hour to solve this one.

World's Hardest "Submarine Net" Puzzle

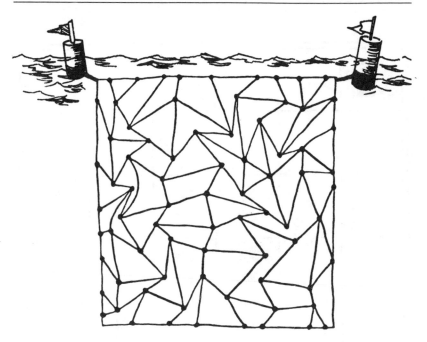

This submarine net, created at the turn of the century, was used to combat the menace of the new underseas submersibles. To counter this threat, Monsieur Gamonet from France invented his famous underwater diving suit. Using this device, see if you can divide the net in two, from top to bottom, with the fewest number of cuts. None of the cuts may be through the knots. Suit up and start snipping.

World's Hardest "Marbles" Puzzle

When it comes to the cutthroat world of school-yard marbles in Cleveland, Thumbs Thurston is the lad to beat. His collection of "aggies," "glassies," "alleys," "baries," and "puries" is second to none. As you can see, his pouch is filled to overflowing. Yesterday, after cleaning out the sixth grade, Thumbs counted up his loot. He found that if he divided his marbles up into groups of twos, threes, fours, fives, and sixes, he always had one marble left over. However, if he divided them into groups of seven, none were left over. What is the least number of marbles Thumbs could have had to achieve these results?

World's Hardest "Will" Puzzle

"And to my beloved family, who have waited so long for this moment, I bequeath the following:

'What does man love e'en more than life,
Hate more than death or mortal strife?
That which contented men desire,
The poorest have and the rich require,
The miser spends and the spendthrift saves,
And all men carry to their graves.'"

The will of the Earl of Eastwich, some centuries ago, was certainly colorful. Can you figure out from the poem what his lordship gave his heirs?

World's Hardest "Film" Puzzle

When Grandpa Townsend was a young man, he bought a new Kodak Iris Diaphragm Shutter camera for Christmas. The camera had a super film capacity. When Grandpa counted up all relatives present, he found that if he took four pictures of each relative, he needed a second roll of film because he ran four photos over the number that fit on a film roll. However, if he took only three photos of each relative, twelve unexposed frames would be left on the original roll. How many relatives did Grandpa have to photograph, and how many photos could he shoot from one roll? You should solve this one in a flash.

World's Hardest "Distance" Puzzle

Yukon Ned is shown here crossing Loon Lake on his sled-mobile. He left his mining camp to pick up his monthly supplies in Nome. Ned was sledding along at a steady 12 miles per hour when his sled broke down halfway to Nome. Ned then travelled the next two miles on foot in a half-hour. Ned then hitched a ride on a passing dogsled and finished his journey to Nome at the rate of 8 miles per hour. The whole trip took Ned one and a half hours from his camp to the Nome general store. Can you figure out what the *distance* was from his camp to the store?

World's Hardest "Toast" Puzzle

Back in the 1920s a new kind of electric toaster was manufactured. It could toast two slices of bread at once, but it only toasted one side of the bread at a time. First, you'd put the bread in the toaster, and after 30 seconds, you'd turn the slices over to toast them for another 30 seconds on the other side. Now here's our problem. Dick and Jane were in a hurry and wanted to toast three slices of bread for breakfast. How could they do it in less than two minutes?

World's Hardest "Toothpick" Puzzle

Doctor Stall and Professor Quackenbush are having dinner at the Toronto Inn and amusing themselves with after-dinner toothpick puzzles. Doctor Stall has laid out an equation using Roman numerals. The equation is incorrect, but he claims that by shifting just one toothpick to a new position, he can correct it. Professor Quackenbush is not so sure about that. Can you pick out the correct move?

World's Hardest "Billiard Ball" Puzzle

Pockets Prendergast, Idle Hours Billiard Academy impresario, has a hundred ways of parting clientele from their cash. One of his favorites is shown above. He lines up eight billiard balls, alternating a colored object ball with a white cue ball. He'll bet that in four moves you can't end up with the four white balls on the left and the four colored balls on the right in a row. During each move, you must move any two *adjacent* balls to a new position in the row. Let's see if you can solve this one before Pockets runs the table.

World's Hardest "Haystacks" Puzzle

Last week it was hayin' time down at Cy Corncrib's farm. Cy had nine haystacks up in the north corner of his hay field, twice that number in the east corner, three times as many in the south corner, and five in the west corner. They spent two days piling it all together in the center of the field. During that time, they had quite a windstorm and the hay from two stacks was scattered all over the field.

When they were *finished*, how many haystacks did they have?

World's Hardest "Keyboard" Puzzle

Neither of these two relics from an office at the turn of the century would be much help in solving this puzzle. We include them here only for atmosphere. What we're interested in is the keyboard of a modern typewriter. The second row from the top contains these letters:

QWERTYUIOP

Our question is simple. What is the longest English word that you can type using only the letters from this row? You may use the letters more than once. If you miss the answer, you'll find yourself asking, "Why didn't I think of that?"

World's Hardest "Doggie" Puzzle

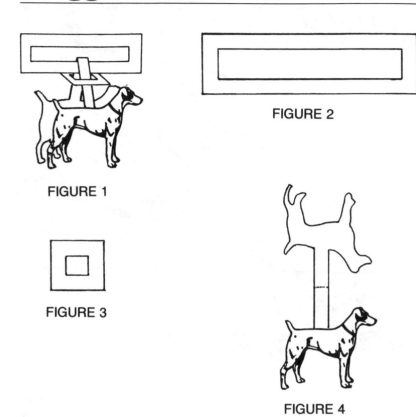

FIGURE 1

FIGURE 2

FIGURE 3

FIGURE 4

This ingenious paper puzzle is dedicated to my dog, Jackie. Figure 1 shows the assembled puzzle. It's constructed of three fairly stiff pieces of paper. Discover how they were put together without tearing or mutilating any of the fragile pieces. Note that the dog is firmly locked onto the large paper link by the smaller paper link. The hole in the small link, however, is far too small for either dog to fit through it. The three pieces that make up the puzzle are shown in figures 2, 3, and 4. See if you can fetch the answer before chow time.

Answers

Answers

Some puzzles have more than one solution. We have given the most common solutions here.

"Radio" Puzzle (page 6). The word is *DOZENS*. Take away one letter, the *S*, and you have *DOZEN*, which of course is twelve.

"Checkbook" Puzzle (page 7). There is no reason why the totals of the two sides of the ledger should ever be the same. The total of the balances on the ledger's right side have nothing to do with a total of the sums withdrawn from the account.

"Checkerboard" Puzzle (page 8). White to move and win: (26 to 22), (18 to 25), (21 to 17), (14 to 21), (19 to 16), (12 to 26), (27 to 31). Black is now completely blocked from moving and, consequently, loses the game.

"Plywood" Puzzle (page 9). Cut along the dotted lines and rearrange as shown.

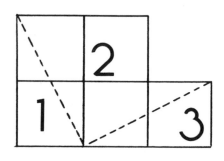 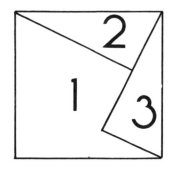

"Western" Puzzle (page 10). Apparently these are two of the most educated gun slingers in the Old West. Their sentences are *palindromes*. That is, the sentences are the same when read backwards or forward. A popular example is "Madam, I'm Adam."

102

"Line" Puzzle (page 11).

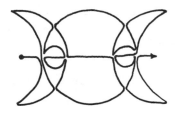

"Flour" Puzzle (page 12). On the first shelf exchange sacks (7) and (2). You now have a single sack (2) and a pair (78). Multiplied together we get 156. We then move single sack (5) and exchange it for sack (9) on the middle shelf. The total number on the middle shelf is now 156. Finally, we move sack (9) from the middle shelf down to shelf three, where it takes the place of sack (4) in the pair. Sack (4) is moved to the right, where it becomes the single sack. Now on shelf three we have (39) times (4), which gives us a product of 156. We did this by moving only five sacks.

"Animal" Puzzle (page 13). Antelope: 22-33-24-25-16-15-14-4, ape: 22-14-6, bear: 55-46-38-47, beaver: 21-29-38-37-46-47, bison: 21-18-10-11-2, boar: 55-65-66-76, bull: 21-20-12-4, calf: 31-22-12-21, camel: 59-69-78-68-60, cat: 45-44-34, deer: 52-51-42-41, doe: 75-67-68, dog: 75-65-56, donkey: 52-43-53-61-71-72, elk: 68-60-61, elephant: 6-16-25-33-32-22-23-24, fox: 21-11-1, giraffe: 56-48-47-38-30-21-29, goat: 56-65-66-74, hare: 57-66-76-68, hen: 81-71-70, heron: 32-42-41-50-49, hog: 57-65-56, horse: 57-67-76-77-68, hyena: 81-72-71-70-69, lamb: 16-7-8-9, leopard: 60-51-50-58-66-76-75, lion: 39-

40-50-49, lynx: 12-3-2-1, mole: 78-79-80-71, monkey: 78-79-70-61-71-72, otter: 43-34-24-25-26, ox: 11-1, panther: 14-22-23-24-32-42-41, pig: 58-48-56, porcupine: 33-43-35-54-63-62-70, rat: 35-44-34, rhinoceros: 47-57-48-49-50-59-68-76-67-77, seal: 77-68-69-60, squirrel: 17-18-27-36-35-26-25-16, tiger: 74-64-56-46-47, toad: 74-65-66-75 or 34-43-44-52, weasel: 5-6-7-17-25-16, wolf: 5-13-12-21.

"Glass" Puzzle (page 14). Before you remove the glass, light the second match. Now, use it to light the head of the match being held by the two glasses. After the head of this match flares up, wait a second or two and blow out the flame. After a few moments, the match should be fused to the glass. Then you can remove the other glass, and the match will remain suspended in air. That's how J. Wellington took the guys down at Bits and Grits Coffee Shop.

"Boat" Puzzle (page 15). After the first crossing was complete, the combined distances travelled by the two boats was equal to twice the width of the river. When the boats met for a second time during the homeward crossing, the total combined distance travelled would then equal three times the width of the river.

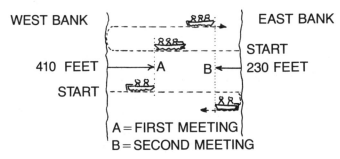

Now, when the boats first met on the river, the sum of the distances each had travelled equaled the width of the river. When they met the second time, each boat would have travelled three times as far as it had travelled when they first had met. During the first meeting, the slower boat had obviously gone 410 feet from shore. When they met the second time, this boat would have gone three times this distance, or 1,230 feet. At the second meeting, the slower boat was 230 feet from the shore. If we subtract this amount from the total distance the slower boat had travelled, we get 1,000 feet for the width of the river.

The time spent on shore has no effect on the outcome of this problem. In this problem the Bennington girls proved to have the faster boat.

"Paper" Puzzle (page 16). The length of the fold is 11.57 inches. The answer can be calculated from the measurements of two right triangles using the Pythagorean theorem (the square of the hypotenuse of a right triangle equals the sum of the squares of the other two sides).

Let's start with the small triangle at point B on the paper (see figure 1). All calculations are rounded to two decimal places. Subtract 10.16 inches from 11 inches, which gives us .84 inches, the side of the small triangle. Now, square .84, which gives us .71 square inches. Square the hypotenuse, 1.38, which gives us 1.90 square inches. Subtract .71 from 1.90, which gives us 1.19 square inches. Taking the square root of this will give us 1.09 inches, the base of the triangle.

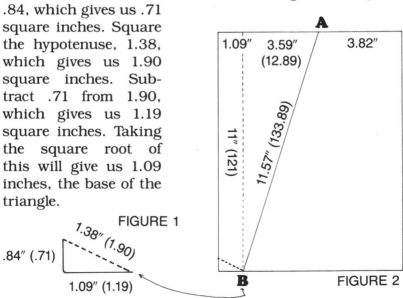

FIGURE 1

FIGURE 2

Square inches are in parentheses.

Now, look at figure 2. Add the 1.09 inches to the 3.82 inches on the right side of the paper, which gives us 4.91 inches. Subtract this 4.91 inches from the paper's width, 8.5 inches, which equals 3.59 inches, the side of our second triangle. Square 3.59 inches, which gives us 12.89 square inches. Square the 11-inch base; that gives us 121 square inches. Add 12.89 and 121 square inches, which equals 133.89 square inches. Then, take the square root of this figure, and you will get the answer to our problem— 11.57 inches for the length of the line A—B.

Harriet should be running the company and not stuck in the secretarial pool, but will Herbert ever be able to swallow his pride?

"Division" Puzzle (page 17).

The Division Puzzle

```
        971
53 ) 51463
     477
      376
      371
       53
       53
```

"Hardware" Puzzle (page 18). Nine washers are equal in weight to one bolt.

"T" Puzzle (page 19).

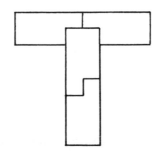

"Age" Puzzle (page 20). Madge is 30 years old; her sister Veronica is 10 years old.

"Chess" Puzzle (page 21).

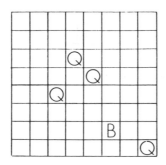

"Card" Puzzle (page 22). The setup of the cards—from top to bottom—is as follows: three, eight, seven, ace, queen, six, four, two, jack, king, ten, nine, and five.

"Antique" Puzzle (page 23). There may be other solutions to this puzzle, but this is the only one the author knows.

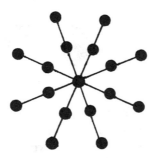

"Archaeology" Puzzle (page 24). The smallest number of blocks needed would be 128. The cube would have four blocks on a side (4 × 4 × 4 = 64 blocks). It would sit on a plaza with eight blocks to a side (8 × 8 = 64). This fulfills the stipulation that one side of the plaza must be twice as long as one side of the cube.

"Brick" Puzzle (page 25). In the two illustrations below, the dotted lines represent the bottom layer of bricks, the solid lines, the second layer.

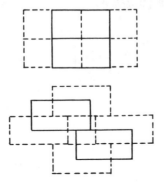

"Escape" Puzzle (page 26). The answer is indeed a snap. When doing this puzzle, always use wooden, not plastic, checkers since wooden checkers will not lock together. Stack the checkers, from the bottom up, as follows: two black checkers, one red checker, and eight to ten black checkers. Now, take the extra red checker and stand it on

end about five inches from the stack. Next, place your first finger on the top edge of the checker and press down hard on it. The checker will shoot out from under your finger, and if it has been aimed correctly, it will strike the red checker—sending it flying out from under the black checkers. The black checkers will, in turn, drop down on top of the bottom two black checkers, leaving the pile intact.

A little practice will make you an expert at this puzzle. It really isn't as hard as it looks.

"Number" Puzzle (page 27).

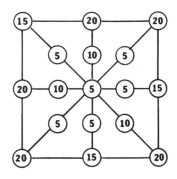

"Dot" Puzzle (page 28).

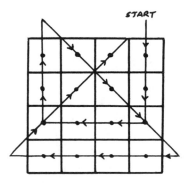

"Castle" Puzzle (page 29). There may be other possible routes, but the one shown here is the one that Edwin of York used successfully for over forty years.

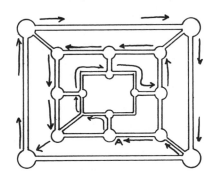

"Rebus" Puzzle (page 30). The answer is: To be always over "confident" in the midst of EXAMS diminishes ("dim" in "ISHES") one's chances for success in them (4 6 s in "THEM").

"Poet" Puzzle (page 31). The poets, in order of the lines in which they appear, are Gray, Moore, Byron, Pope, Dryden, Gay, Keats, and Hemans. Marianne Moore is the sole American poet.

"Floating Paper" Puzzle (page 32). If you bet on this puzzle, you'd better make your first bet a large one because this solution will only work once. Simply take sheet *a* and crumple it into a ball. When released, the crumpled sheet will drop straight down to the floor while sheet *b* will slowly float down.

"Paper Match" Puzzle (page 33).

"Magic Square" Puzzle (page 34).

16	3	2	13
5	10	11	8
9	6	7	12
4	15	14	1

"Soda Straw" Puzzle (page 35). This time, instead of a two-dimensional six-sided figure, we get a three-dimensional six-sided figure. Now isn't that a neat solution?

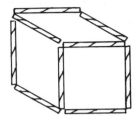

"Newspaper" Puzzle (page 36). To solve this one, we've resorted to a mixture of English and Roman numerals. Devious, but it works.

$$
\begin{array}{rcc}
\text{SIX} & \text{IX} & \text{XL} \\
- \ \ \underline{\text{IX}} & \underline{\text{X}} & \underline{\text{L}} \\
\text{S} & \text{I} & \text{X}
\end{array}
$$

"Steamship " Puzzle (page 37). The next time all three ships will leave New York on the same day is 240 days later. This is the least common multiple of 12, 16, and 20, the number of days each completes a round trip. As for how many round trips each ship makes in this period, the first ship makes 240 ÷ 12 = 20 trips, the second ship makes 240 ÷ 16 = 15 trips, and the third ship makes 240 ÷ 20 = 12 trips.

"Typewriter" Puzzle (page 38). The answer to the doodle words are (1) hang-up, (2) dunderhead, (3) once upon a time, (4) head over heels in love, (5) day in, day out, (6) Sopwith Camel, (7) Unfinished Symphony, and (8) double bed.

"Gold Bar" Puzzle (page 39). The fewest number of pieces needed to cut the bar into are five. The pieces would measure one, two, four, eight, and sixteen inches in length. Using a combination of these five pieces, Patrick could always add an inch of gold to his daily bill at the Northern Lights Saloon. At the end of February and the months with just 30 days, Patrick used leftover gold to tip the waiters and show girls. What class!

"Moon" Puzzle (page 40). The maximum number of space stations that can be built on the moon, under the conditions described, are four. With more than four, it would be impossible for every station to be the same distance from every other station. The drawing shows the locations of these four stations.

"Train" Puzzle (page 41). From the time the locomotive enters the tunnel at one end to the time it leaves the tunnel at the other end, the locomotive will have travelled one mile. However, the rest of the train will still be in the tunnel. The locomotive must travel another mile before the entire train clears the tunnel. Therefore, the train travels two miles before finally clearing the tunnel. Since the train moves at 15 miles an hour, it travels one mile in 4 minutes. So, the total time necessary for the train to completely pass through the tunnel is 8 minutes.

"Chicken" Puzzle (page 42). On a regular day, Amy and Bessie brought in $15.00 and $10.00 for a total of $25.00. When Bessie brought the 60 chickens to market everything went fine until she ran out of Amy's chickens. Two of her chickens, together with three of Amy's, were indeed worth $5.00. However, once Amy's were gone, she had to start selling the remaining ten chickens, which were hers. Since Bessie's chickens were worth $2.50 for five, she lost 50 cents for each of the last two transactions. I hope that she was able to convince Amy that she hadn't been cheated.

"Progression" Puzzle (page 43). The key to the progression is the number 3. You must subtract 3, divide by 3, add 3, subtract 3, divide by 3, add 3, etc. Starting with hole 1, we subtract 3 from 12 and get 9, the score for hole 2. We then divide the 9 by 3 and get 3, the score for hole 3. We then add 3 to 3 to get 6, the score for hole 4. We then subtract 3 from 6 to get 3, the score for hole 5. We then divide 3 by 3 to get 1, the score for hole 6. Finally, for hole 7, we add 3 to 1, the score for hole 6. Finally, for hole 7, we add 3 to 1 to get 4, the answer to the problem.

"Coin" Puzzle (page 44). The smallest number of coins needed to pay the exact cost of any item from one cent through one dollar is nine. The coins are: 4 pennies, 1 nickel, 2 dimes, 1 quarter, and 1 half dollar.

"Clairvoyant" Puzzle (page 45). This is one of those tricky bets. After staring intently at the back of the coin, you give your audience the current date. After all, you simply promised to tell them the date. You never said you'd reveal the date on the coin. Keep the bet small so your friends don't get too mad at you.

"Logo" Puzzle (page 46). First, fold a sheet of paper as shown in figure 1. Next, draw the three connecting lines.

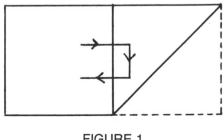

FIGURE 1

Now, without moving the pen, unfold the paper as shown in figure 2. You can now complete the logo without going over any line more than once and without lifting the pen from the paper.

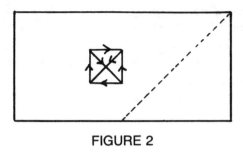

FIGURE 2

"Dumbbell" Puzzle (page 47). Basil had seven dumbbells and Bertie had five dumbbells.

"Rug" Puzzle (page 48). He cut along the dotted lines shown in figure 1. Then he shifted the top half of the rug to the left and down, where it neatly fitted into the bottom half of the rug (figure 2). A few deft stitches with the old needle and thread and Abdul had sewn a perfect carpet before sundown.

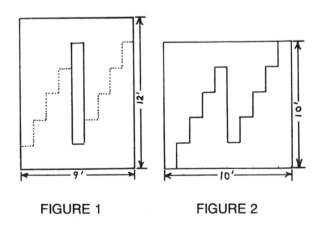

FIGURE 1   FIGURE 2

"Gulliver" Puzzle (page 49). The five "little airy creatures" hidden in the poem are the vowels *a*, *e*, *i*, *o*, and *u*.

You'll find *a* in the word *glass*, *e* in the word *jet*, *i* in the word *tin*, *o* in the word *box*, and *u* in the word *you*. Swift called them airy because their sound is formed by air passing over the vocal cords when you say them.

"Lawn" Puzzle (page 50). Looking at the diagram, we can see first that the ram can graze through an area that is ¾ of a circle with a 60-foot radius. This can be expressed:

.75 × pi (3.14159) × radius (60 feet) squared
.75 × 3.14159 × 60 × 60 = 8,482.29 square feet

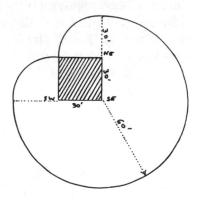

Next, the ram can graze through two smaller areas at the southwest and northeast corners of the property. Each of these areas is one-fourth the area of a circle with a radius of 30 feet. This can be expressed:

.50 × pi (3.14159) × radius (30 feet) squared
.50 × 3.14159 × 30 × 30 = 1,413.71 square feet

Thus, the total area that Amos can munch over is:

8,482.29 + 1,413.71 = 9,896 square feet, approximately.

The answer will vary slightly, of course, depending on the value of pi (whether rounded off or given with as many as 8 digits right of the decimal point).

"Political" Puzzle (page 51). Starting with the *T* on the left side, at the bottom of the frame, read around the frame clockwise. The campaign slogan comes from the 1840 presidential election when William Henry Harrison ran against Martin Van Buren. It was "Tippecanoe and Tyler, Too." *Tippecanoe* was a river in Indiana where Harrison fought some Native Americans, and *Tyler* was John Tyler, his vice-presidential running mate on the Whig ticket. The Harrison—Tyler ticket won.

"Clock" Puzzle (page 52). In one solution, the total time Waldo would have had to wait is one and a half hours. This would happen if he had been awakened by a single chime at 12:15, followed by single chimes at 12:30, 12:45, 1:00, 1:15, 1:30 and 1:45. When he heard the seventh consecutive single chime he knew that it had to be 1:45.

In the other solution, Waldo could have been awakened by the last chime of 12:00. In this case, he would have to wait a full hour and three-quarters before he could be sure of the correct time.

"Math" Puzzle (page 53). If you turn the addition problem upside down, you find that the numbers once again add up to 5,074. The *6*'s become *9*'s, the *9*'s become *6*'s, and the *1*'s and *8*'s stay the same. All in all, this makes an interesting little problem.

"Toy Box" Puzzle (page 54). The length was 12 inches, the width 10 inches, and the height 8 inches.

"Punctuation" Puzzle (page 55). It was "and" I said, not "are," and "and" and "are" are different!

"Sports" Puzzle (page 56). The outdoor sports are (1) CROQUET, (2) SOCCER, (3) BOCCIE, (4) FOOTBALL, (5) VOLLEYBALL, (6) TENNIS, (7) LACROSSE, (8) RACING, (9) STEEPLECHASE, (10) SHOOTING, (11) ARCHERY, (12) BOBSLEDDING, (13) HOCKEY, (14) SAILING, (15) SKAT-

ING, (16) FISHING, (17) BIKING, (18) BALLOONING, (19) BASEBALL, (20) QUOITS, (21) HANDBALL, (22) RUGBY, (23) CRICKET, and (24) SWIMMING.

"Balancing" Puzzle (page 57). Like all great puzzles, the answer is simple—just bend the paper match in half before dropping it. It will then come to rest on its narrow edge when dropped from any height.

"Word" Puzzle (page 58). The word that Barlowe came up with is *attenuate* (at-ten-u-ate).

"King" Puzzle (page 59). The king was *David*. In Roman numerals *500* was "D." The first of all letters is *A*, and the first of all figures (Roman numerals, again) is *I*. Finally, five in the middle is *V*. Put them together and you have *DAVID*.

"Racing" Puzzle (page 60). The professor should bet as follows: $12 on Sway Belly, $15 on Aunt Sara, and $20 on Thunder Hooves. Of course, if any other horse comes in first, the professor is out of luck.

"Barrel" Puzzle (page 61). The barrel containing beer is the one marked 20 gallons. The barrels of wine that went to Ye Olde Ale House are marked 18 gallons and 15 gallons. The barrels that banker Rumport bought are marked 16, 19, and 31 gallons. This means that the ale house received 33 gallons of wine, and the banker bought twice as much—66 gallons. All barrels were present and accounted for.

"Nationality" Puzzle (page 62). Myra was indicating that the lady was *Singhalese* (single *E*'s). Did we catch you on that one?

"Route" Puzzle (page 63). This solution is the one that this author knows. There may be others.

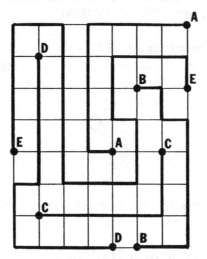

"Inspirational" Puzzle (page 64). And the message is: "To be overtenacious in the midst of trifles is the mark of a mean understanding."

"Backwards" Puzzle (page 65). There may be other sports where you have to move backwards to win, but we came up with three: rowing (sculling in particular), the backstroke race in swimming, and the good old tug-of-war. Did you get them all?

"Odd Figure" Puzzle (page 66). The puzzle calls for arranging five odd *figures* so that they will add up to 14. A *figure* is a numerical value—in this case 1, 3, 5, 7, and 9. So, two *1*'s can be written as eleven. Therefore, the answer can be expressed:

$$
\begin{array}{r}
11 \\
1 \\
1 \\
\underline{1} \\
14
\end{array}
$$

"Hopscotch" Puzzle (page 67). What makes this puzzle so hard is that you must start at point X or at point Y. Did you chalk up a win on this one?

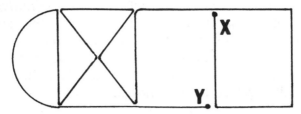

"Wooden Match" Puzzle (page 68). If we used the matches to form an equilateral triangle, the area within the triangle would be 8 inches times 6 inches divided by two, which is 24 inches ($8'' \times 6'' \div 2 = 24''$). By stepping four of the matches in, as shown in the diagram, we drop 12 square inches of area, which leaves us with an enclosed area of 12 square inches, the solution required.

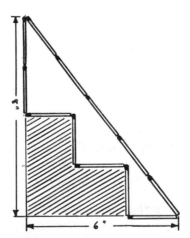

"Circle" Puzzle (page 69). Substitute the following numbers for letters: a = 2, b = 11, c = 8, d = 1, e = 14, f = 4, h = 13, i = 5, and j = 9.

"Letter Dropping" Puzzle (page 70). The letter-dropping sequence is as follows: STARTLING, STARLING, STARING, STRING, STING, SING, SIN, IN, I.

"Bread" Puzzle (page 71). Since the bread was consumed equally by the three men, then each one ate 2⅔ loaves. That means that the native with three loaves to start with only gave up ⅓ of a loaf to Forsythe, while the native with five loaves gave up 2⅓ loaves. This native then gave up seven times as much bread as the first native, so he was entitled to seven coins and the first native to one coin. This is the fair solution to the problem. Whether the natives actually arrived at it or not, we shall never know.

"Roller" Puzzle (page 72). If you said 22 inches, you're wrong. When the roller has made one revolution, the air-conditioning unit will have moved forward a distance equal to two circumferences of the roller. Don't forget that as the roller moves the unit forward, the roller is also moving forward. The answer is 43.982 inches, and the formula is $2 \times pi (3.14159) \times 7$ inches (diameter of roller) = 43.982.

"Safe" Puzzle (page 73). Timothy must have had a bad memory indeed, if he couldn't remember 37—37—37.

$$37 \times 3 = 111. \quad 37 \times 6 = 222. \quad 37 \times 9 = 333.$$

"Money" Puzzle (page 74). The first pile contains 88 coins and the second pile contains 12. One-fourth of 88 is 22, which is 20 more than 2, which is one-sixth of 12.

"Transposition" Puzzle (page 75). The 22 moves are: 10 to 5, 1 to 8, 11 to 6, 2 to 9, 12 to 7, 3 to 4, 5 to 12, 8 to 3, 6 to 1, 9 to 10, 7 to 6, 4 to 9, 12 to 7, 3 to 4, 1 to 8, 10 to 5, 6 to 1, 9 to 10, 7 to 2, 4 to 11, 8 to 3, 5 to 12.

"Poker Chip" Puzzle (page 76). The most even rows that can be formed that we know about are 16. The drawing below shows their placement. It's possible to arrange them differently, but the results will be the same.

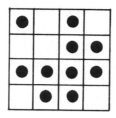

"Target" Puzzle (page 77). First, lay out the 18 scoring shots into three groups of six scores, with each group totaling 71 points.

Alexander	25,	20,	20,	3,	2,	1
Sybilla	25,	20,	10,	10,	5,	1
Swanhilda	50,	10,	5,	3,	2,	1

The first set of numbers must belong to Alexander, because that set is the only one that contains two numbers that add up to 22.

The third set of numbers has to belong to Swanhilda because it is the only one that contains a 3. Therefore, Swanhilda scored the 50-point bull's-eye.

"Square" Puzzle (page 78).

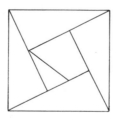

"Baseball" Puzzle (page 79). The answer is simple. It was a game between two girls' baseball teams, so, of course, no *man* ever got to third base. The winning run came from a homer by Betty the Blaster.

"What?" Puzzle (page 80). (1) the letter *n*, (2) a yardstick, (3) a police car, (4) a lawsuit, (5) music.

"Moving" Puzzle (page 81). First, light the fourth match, and then use it to light the heads of the three upright matches. Quickly extinguish the flames of all four matches. You will find that the heads of the pyramid matches have fused together, so that you can easily lift them from the table with the fourth match.

"Bottle" Puzzle (page 82). To be successful, you must use a bare table, with no cloth on it, and make sure that you place the coin no more than two inches from the edge. Now, if you're right-handed, place a table knife, with its blade flat on the table, to the right of the coin. Sharply sweep the knife blade to the left against the coin, knocking it out from under the bottle. Continue sweeping the knife to the left, so that you do not touch the bottle as it descends. Inertia will keep the bottle from tipping over as it drops the short distance to the table top. You'll need a little practice, but soon you'll be an expert at presenting this puzzle.

If you're left-handed, you'll be sweeping the knife blade to the right.

"Cork" Puzzle (page 83). Fill the glass nearly to the top, and then place the cork in the water. Now, carefully pour more water into the glass until the water level is slightly above the glass's rim. If done with care, the surface tension of the liquid will allow the water to form a slightly convex shape. The cork will then "float" uphill to the center of the glass and stay there.

"Weighty" Puzzle (page 84). The word that will allow the professor to toddle off to bed is *TON*. Read forward it's a heavy word, and when read backwards it's *NOT*.

"Rectangle" Puzzle (page 85). You can draw 20 rectangles using the 12 black dots in the illustration. The two that everyone seems to miss are shown here. I hope that you didn't miss them.

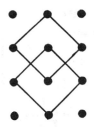

"Ballooning" Puzzle (page 86). The word hanging from the right balloon that should be moved over to the left balloon is . . . *DUNE*. All the words on the left can be preceded by *SAND*. Thus we have *SANDBAG, SANDBANK, SANDSTORM,* and *SANDBAR*. Add *DUNE* and we get *SANDDUNE*.

"Brothers" Puzzle (page 87). The Gundersons were two brothers from a set of triplets. How do you like the delivery on that one?

"Suitcase" Puzzle (page 88). The Frontenacs placed two objects inside the suitcase. In the half that hung over the table edge, they placed a large piece of pig iron. At the other end of the case, they placed a large block of ice. The weight of the ice, plus the leverage gained by its being placed over the table, more than offset the pig iron's weight. However, as the ice melted, the water became evenly distributed throughout the suitcase, which caused the end with the pig iron to become heavy enough to tip the case off of the table. This was certainly one of the most novel timing devices used in the entertainment world.

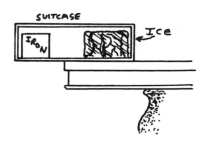

"A to Z" Puzzle (page 89).

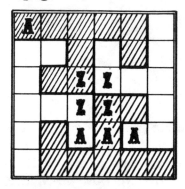

"Submarine Net" Puzzle (page 90). The fewest number of cuts needed to divide the net in two is eight. Starting at Section *A*, snip your way down to section *B*.

"Marbles" Puzzle (page 91). Thumbs's bag contained 301 marbles.

"Will" Puzzle (page 92). I'm afraid that the earl was more extravagant than anyone thought. It seems that he left his heirs . . . *nothing*.

"Film" Puzzle (page 93). That Christmas, Grandpa Townsend invited 16 relatives over, and one roll of the new super Kodak film allowed him to take 60 pictures.

"Distance" Puzzle (page 94). The distance from Ned's camp to the general store was 12 miles.

"Toast" Puzzle (page 95). First, they put two slices in the toaster and turned it on. After 30 seconds, they turned over the first slice, took out the second slice, and put in the third. After another 30 seconds, the first slice was done on both sides, and slices two and three were half-done. They took out the first slice, put the second slice back in and turned over the third slice. After another 30 seconds, all three slices were toasted on both sides for a total toasting time of one and a half minutes. Pass the butter and marmalade, please.

"Toothpick" Puzzle (page 96). Shift the single toothpick on the right of the equals sign left to make the minus into a plus sign (6 + 4 = 10) *or* shift the single toothpick from the number 6 to create a plus sign from the original minus sign (5 + 4 = 9).

"Billiard Ball" Puzzle (page 97). The following four-move combination is a sure winner.

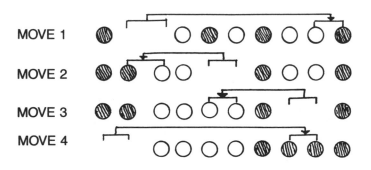

"Haystacks" Puzzle (page 98). If you said one, you're right on the money. They piled all the hay in the middle of the field in one big stack.

"Keyboard" Puzzle (page 99). The answer we were looking for is *TYPEWRITER*, but there are a few more ten-letter words that you can type from this single row of keys.

"Doggie" Puzzle (page 100). Fold the large link (b) in figure 1, and slip the small link over the end marked *d*. Now, hang the dog on the link as shown in figure 1, and slip the small link back over the end (d), then down onto the dog. Open up the large link and the puzzle is finished (figure 2). Hint: When you fold the large link just bend it; do not crease it. That way, when you open it out, there will be no indication that the large link was ever folded.

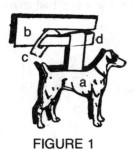

FIGURE 1

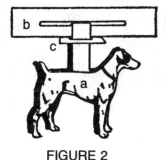

FIGURE 2

Index

About the Author

Charles Barry Townsend has been writing books on puzzles, games, and magic for over 17 years. He is the author of twelve books, including *The World's Best Puzzles*, *The World's Most Challenging Puzzles*, *The World's Toughest Puzzles*, *The World's Most Baffling Puzzles*, and *The World's Best Magic Tricks*, all published by Sterling. He lives in Hilton Head, South Carolina, where he spends a good deal of his time thinking up ways to confound and entertain readers like you.

Find the **"Doggie" Puzzle** on page 106.